Original title:
A Taste of the Tropics

Copyright © 2025 Creative Arts Management OÜ
All rights reserved.

Author: Giselle Montgomery
ISBN HARDBACK: 978-1-80581-511-2
ISBN PAPERBACK: 978-1-80581-038-4
ISBN EBOOK: 978-1-80581-511-2

Driftwood Tales Along Sandy Shores

Driftwood dances in the breeze,
A coconut sings as it flees,
Seagulls squawk in silly flight,
Chasing crabs that run with fright.

Palm trees stand with hands on hips,
Laughing at the ocean's dips,
Turtles tumble, surfboard spies,
While starfish wear their sunny ties.

The Sweetness of Island Harvests

Mangoes bounce from tree to ground,
Pineapples roll without a sound,
Coconuts giggle in the sun,
Yelling, 'Come! Let's have some fun!'

Bananas wear a slip and slide,
As papayas seek a place to hide,
Together they form a fruity crew,
Sipping juice with a tropical view.

Twilight Glow on Sugary Sands

The sun dips low with a cheeky grin,
Sandy toes dance, let the fun begin,
A crab wears shades and strikes a pose,
Waves applaud with a splash that glows.

Stars twinkle like sprinkles on a cake,
Jellyfish jiggle, oh what a break,
Beach balls soar with a woosh and a plop,
As the laughter never seems to stop.

Memories Tucked in Hibiscus Blooms

Hibiscus blooms in colors bright,
Sharing secrets of the night,
They giggle low in sunny cliques,
Telling tales of silly tricks.

Butterflies twirl in flower hats,
Dancing with the chattering chats,
Honey bees play hide and seek,
Buzzing jokes in vibrant peaks.

The Lush Embrace of Paradise

In a jungle gym of green, oh what a sight,
Where monkeys swing and party all night.
Coconuts fall with a thud, what a clunk,
The squirrels look startled, then do a funky dunk.

The parrots squawk jokes with vibrant cheer,
While chubby iguanas munch on some beer.
A toucan struts like a true diva star,
Saying, "This fiesta's the best near and far!"

Mangoes & Moonlit Nights

Under the stars with a mango delight,
Juice drips down my chin, what a sticky sight!
I danced with a crab, who had two left feet,
He offered me snacks, we shared quite a treat.

The moon laughed loud at our silly chance,
As I tripped on a shell while attempting to dance.
A mango pit flew—oh, a laugh it did spark,
"Watch out!" cried a fish, "you'll dent my newark!"

Whispering Palms

Whispering palms with secrets to share,
Tell of a parrot who dyed his own hair.
He claimed to be hip, with style so supreme,
But really he looked like a tropical dream!

The coconuts chuckle at all his flair,
Saying, "Come on now, we've seen better hair!"
A crab with a hat joined in on the fun,
"Let's start a band," he yelled, "we'll be number one!"

Tropical Reverie

In a hammock of dreams under skies so bright,
I snoozed through a duel between day and night.
Lying there laughing as crabs tried to prance,
Their awkward attempts were a sight for a dance!

A pineapple hat and some flip-flops on me,
I joined in the fun at a bouncy sea spree.
The dolphins were diving, the sea turtles glared,
"Please don't ask us to join, we're slightly impaired!"

Sunkissed Delights

Pineapples dancing in the sun,
Bananas slip by, oh what fun!
Coconuts giggle from the trees,
While mangoes tease the gentle breeze.

Limes wear shades, looking so cool,
Lemons laugh, 'Who needs a pool?'
Papayas throw a tropical bash,
But one too many leads to a splash!

Fragrant Shores of Paradise

Coconuts roll like tumbleweeds,
While marigolds spill laughter's seeds.
The ocean waves wear a scented dress,
And seagulls dance in sheer excess.

Crabs in tuxedos strut on the sand,
While seashells gossip, hand in hand.
A fish in sunglasses swims on by,
Saying, 'Who needs to dry? Oh my!'

Lush Whispers of the Breeze

The palm trees gossip with a sway,
Telling stories of a bright, sunny day.
Flowers chuckle, pointing with glee,
At a lizard attempting to climb a tree.

The breeze plays tricks, pulls hats away,
While flip-flops frolic in a funny ballet.
A little toucan steals the scene,
Wearing a tutu, looking quite keen!

Chasing Sunbeams and Coconut Dreams

Sunbeams racing through the sky,
While lazy clouds drift by, oh my!
Coconut drinks with little umbrellas,
Charming all the beachside fellas.

Tropical birds sing songs of cheer,
While beach balls bounce without fear.
Friends in hammocks giggle aloud,
As beach chairs form a lounging crowd!

The Aroma of Salted Air

The ocean waves are on a spree,
They tickle my toes and shout with glee.
Seagulls squawk, they steal my fries,
I laugh and throw them a surprise.

The breeze brings scents of coconut pie,
As I try to dodge that pesky fly.
Sandy shoes and salty hair,
I dance like no one's watching—take care!

Sunkissed Shores

The sun's a chef with a frying pan,
Cooking up fun, oh, what a plan!
Beachballs bounce like a wild parade,
While I'm buried in this sunbaked shade.

With flip-flops squeaking, I strut my stuff,
The wave's a joker, "You're not tough!"
I slip and slide, a comical sight,
In this sandy circus, I feel just right.

Veils of Tropical Rain

The rain arrives but oh, what charm,
Each drop's a tickle, no cause for alarm.
Puddles form where I take my stand,
Splashing joyfully, my own wonderland.

Umbrellas flip as if they're mad,
I laugh so hard, it's a bit bad!
Drenched to the bone, I crank up the fun,
In this playful storm, I'm never done.

Evening in Eden

As night falls like a giant blanket,
The stars peep out; do they prank or pranket?
With fireflies twinkling, they're on the job,
In this garden, I'm a dancing mob.

The critters join with their own sound bites,
A kooky choir of goofy delights.
Laughter echoes under the moon's shy glow,
This mystical eve is quite the show!

A Palette Dipped in Sunshine

Pineapple hats on monkeys dance,
Coconuts sing, they take a chance,
Limes in shorts, all kick and sway,
Mangoes giggle, joy on display.

Bananas slide, a peel parade,
Papayas joke, they've got it made,
Orange ballads in the breeze,
Laughter echoes through the trees.

Essences of the Tropic

A parrot squawks, wearing shades,
Tropical drinks in comical raids,
Kiwis in flip-flops, wiggling toes,
While drumming pineapples steal the show.

Cactus joins, under sun's embrace,
Jellyfish jig in a jelly race,
Silly mango mustaches abound,
Nature's jokes in colors profound.

The Alchemy of Island Fruits

Coconuts crack with giddy cheer,
While starfruit twinkles, oh so dear,
Lime slice hats on tropical sprites,
Making magic on sunny nights.

Bananas glance, a slapstick scene,
Bouncing mangoes, bright and keen,
Kiwi cousins chuckle so sweet,
As fruit cocktails tap their feet.

Oasis of Dreams

Welcome to where laughter flows,
Grapes in goggles, say hello!
Watermelons play peek-a-boo,
As cherry bombs make quite a crew.

Fragrant flowers join the fun,
Dancing under the blazing sun,
Coconut clowns with jolly glee,
In this dreamland, wild and free.

Tropical Symphony in Bloom

In the garden, bugs take flight,
They dance and buzz, such a sight.
A parrot squawks a silly tune,
While monkeys throw bananas soon.

Coconut trees sway with glee,
A chorus of leaves, wild and free.
A pineapple joins with a grin,
While lizards leap in laughter's din.

Bright flowers laugh in colors bold,
As sticky honey drips like gold.
The sun sings songs of fruity cheer,
With laughter echoing year to year.

So raise a toast to nature's jest,
In this paradise, we feel the best.
With every giggle, we proclaim,
This tropical fun is life's great game.

Beneath the Palms' Embrace

Beneath the palms, a crab trots by,
Wearing sunglasses, oh my!
A sunbathing snail takes its time,
Sipping lemonade, feeling sublime.

The breeze tells jokes, a witty breeze,
While sandy turtles crawl with ease.
A gecko cracks a pun or two,
Flipping its tail in a funny view.

Coconuts roll like little balls,
While the distant ocean calls.
Crickets chirp their nighttime song,
Joining in the fun all night long.

So here we laugh beneath the trees,
In this paradise, we're at ease.
With giggles shared round the shore,
Life's a comedy, who could ask for more?

Mango Moonlit Serenade

The mango moon begins to glow,
A dancing fruit, oh what a show!
As coconuts start to jive,
With rhythm that makes us feel alive.

Pineapples wear sombreros bright,
And swing their tops with pure delight.
Watermelons roll and sway,
Making merry in a fruity way.

A chorus of frogs croaks out a tune,
Underneath the watchful moon.
Sea turtles join in with a clap,
All nature's critters in a happy scrap.

So let's all waltz in tropical bliss,
With mango magic we can't miss.
In this moonlit serenade we find,
A joyful rhythm, heart and mind.

Dancing with the Waves

The ocean waves do the cha-cha,
As crabs applaud with a hurrah!
A fish in flip-flops joins the fun,
While seagulls squawk, 'We've just begun!'

Sandy feet tap to the beat,
A dance of joy and summer heat.
Beach balls bounce from side to side,
As joyful laughter cannot hide.

The tide brings jokes on the shore,
Making us laugh and wanting more.
With each splash, we're filled with glee,
This wild dance is pure jubilee.

So let the waves sway us along,
In this seaside party, we belong.
With every twirl and playful quake,
We celebrate the joy we make.

Hibiscus Dreams

In a hammock we sway, life feels so grand,
With birds in our hair and sand on our hand.
The sun on our faces, sweet drinks in tow,
Unbothered by worries, just enjoying the show.

The flowers are laughing, they look quite absurd,
One's getting tipsy from all the sweet bird.
A coconut falls, it shouts, 'I'm the king!'
While someone's yelling, 'Please, don't bring me that sting!'

The Sweetness of Sunsets

Mangoes are dancing as the day fades out,
While toucans squawk, a joyful shout.
The sky's painted orange, bright as a clown,
While crabs do the cha-cha, wearing their crowns.

The breeze tells a joke, though we can't understand,
It tickles our toes, take my funny hand!
The sun winks at us, cheeky and bold,
As we munch on puffs of sweet coconut gold.

Sipping Paradise

With straws like a band, we're ready to slurp,
A parade of flavors, oh what a chirp!
A papaya froth, with a twist of lime,
We smile at the blender, it's party time!

The ice cubes are chattering, having some fun,
While tiny umbrellas whisper secrets to sun.
"Oh, come on!" yells a pineapple, 'Don't let it freeze!'
Then all join the chorus, "We're here for the tease!"

Waves of Fruitful Delight

The waves crash and giggle, splashing us right,
With pineapples surfing under the moonlight.
Limes in the ocean, laughing up high,
While bananas conspire to steal the sky.

Coconut shells dance, they call out for fun,
"Hey, juicy mango, let's run 'til we're done!"
The seashells are clapping, creating a beat,
As we jive with the fruits, life tastes so sweet!

Solstice in Paradise

In the sun, my drink's a mess,
It's filled with fruit, but what a stress!
A parrot steals my mango slice,
Sips my rum, oh, that was nice!

The beach towel's now a sail,
With a wasp caught in the trail.
I chase the bird, I'm feeling bold,
He laughs at me, a sight to behold!

Palm trees itch like crazy tricks,
Sandy toes and guava licks.
I'm dancing with my flip-flop mate,
He slips and falls—oh, what a fate!

So cheers to summer, my friend dear,
Let's raise a glass, we've naught to fear.
For as we laugh, the sun won't quit,
This funny life, oh, isn't it!

Echoes of the Tropics

In the jungle, I hear a croak,
A frog that thinks he's quite the bloke.
He serenades, but it's off-key,
Dances like he's run on spree!

Coconuts drop with a loud thud,
Cracking jokes as they hit the mud.
A monkey chuckles from the vine,
He steals my fruit—now that's not fine!

The ocean waves just mock my flip,
While I fumble, trying to skip.
A crab approaches, pinches my toe,
Oh snap, that's a funny show!

Yet amidst the laughs and the bites,
We soak in sun and starry nights.
With echoes loud, we grin and jest,
In this strange paradise, we're blessed!

The Serenade of Coconut Shells

A coconut band plays a tune,
While I try dancing under the moon.
My hips sway wildly, full of cheer,
But I'm stepping on my own foot, dear!

The shells they sing, a clumsy beat,
With everyone's laughter, life's a treat.
The palms swing low, while I stomp high,
Rained on by juice from the sky.

Bananas join in, all aglow,
Complain that my rhythm's rather slow.
But I just laugh, shrug off the fall,
After all, I'm giving my all!

So here's to fun, my fruity friends,
With coconut shells, the laughter never ends.
A silly jig beneath palm leaves,
In this crazy moment, my heart believes!

Sunset's Golden Splash

The sun dips low in a splashy burst,
I trip on my towel, oh, such a thirst!
My drink flies out, a glorious arc,
It lands on a shark—oh, how it spark!

Seagulls giggle at my plight,
As I scramble, what a sight!
I chase my drink, it rolls away,
Of all the games, this one's cliché.

With a sunset that steals the show,
My friend and I can't help but glow.
As fish throw confetti from below,
We toast to missteps, let laughter grow!

So let the waves be wild and free,
In sunset colors, we'll just be glee.
As night falls down with twinkling stars,
We'll laugh at life, and all its wars!

Wrapped in Tropical Splendor

Beneath the sun, we sway and glide,
With coconut hats and aloha pride.
Bananas dance in the palm tree shade,
While my sandwich dreams begin to fade.

A mango slipped on the kitchen floor,
It rolled away—who could ask for more?
Pineapples giggle with each sweet bite,
Say hello to my fruity delight!

Strawberries wear tiny swim trunks tight,
Watermelon sunbathing—what a sight!
Lemonade waves from its glassy throne,
Shouting, "Chill out!" in a tropical tone.

So join the feast, let the laughter flow,
With fruit in hand, we steal the show.
In this paradise, let's make a scene,
With giggles and snacks, living the dream!

Fruits of the Sea

In the bay, crabs do the cha-cha,
While fish debate the best piña colada.
Octopus juggling with eight wiggly arms,
Sardines gossip about all their charms.

Clams express their shell-shocking glee,
As seaweed waves like it's at a spree.
Tropical breezes tickle the tide,
While coconut shells all take a ride.

Shrimp and scallops throw a wild bash,
With a salsa rhythm, they move and dash.
The big fish makes a splash, what a scene,
Proving seafood parties are fit for a queen!

So raise your glasses of sea salt mist,
Here's to the ocean with bubbles and twists.
In this fishy frolic, let's celebrate,
Our seafood soiree, it's purely first rate!

The Flavor of Borders Uncrossed

Mango hats and coconut shoes,
Chasing parrots spreading the blues.
A piña colada in my hand,
Hoping the blender can understand.

Jumping over the neighbor's fence,
For fruit so sweet, it's pure suspense.
I brought guavas; he brought limes,
We barter fruit like it's olden times.

Salsa dancing with my cat on the floor,
He twirls and trips; oh, the uproar!
Bamboo dancers in the yard, a joke,
Turns out, most are just folks in cloaks.

Tropical skies in a sandwich place,
Lettuce hats in a funny race.
Chili peppers play hide and seek,
Leave your worries; let's sneak a peak!

Glistening Isles

Sunlight sparkles on the bay,
Fish wear sunglasses, hippos sway.
Coconuts wear swirly wigs,
While squawking birds show off their digs.

Crabs in tuxedos strut their stuff,
But jellyfish say, 'Isn't that enough?'
Seashells whisper on the shore,
'Is that a fridge? No, it's a door!'

In the sand, we build a castle,
Yes, it's tall, though it may wrassle.
Hermit crabs in a chariot race,
Dodging waves with a twist of grace.

Pirates paint their faces bright,
At brunch they serve a funny sight.
With pancakes flying high and free,
Who knew breakfast could a party be?

The Heartbeat of a Tropical Breeze

Breezes whisper through palm trees,
Tickling cheeks with playful tease.
Air filled with laughter, oh so grand,
Where no one cares about the sand.

Coconut bandits on the run,
Stealing snacks to share with fun.
A toucan perched upon a drum,
Counting beats till the next day's sun.

Swaying hips of mango trees,
Dancing with the shimmying breeze.
Bamboo flutes play a silly tune,
As lizards groove beneath the moon.

Sunsets spill in colors bright,
Kites soaring in a dizzy flight.
Fireflies join the evening cheer,
Their tiny lights spread joy, my dear!

Velvet Nights Under Palm Trees

Velvet nights, the stars do twinkle,
The waves below kick like a sprinkle.
Palm trees gossip with the moon,
While the crickets play a funky tune.

Dancing shadows on the floor,
Monkey suits left at the door.
Banana boats float on dreams,
As laughter bubbles, or so it seems.

Cocktails wobble on our heads,
Like a marching band of roguish treads.
Tiki torches wiggle with delight,
As pineapple pops steal the night.

In dreams, we ride a chubby bear,
Happily unaware of our hair.
With each twist, the world spins fast,
Yet here in fun, we'll always last!

Rhythms of the Rainforest

The monkeys dance, oh what a sight,
Swinging and twirling, with pure delight.
Parrots squawk, they join the fun,
In this green place, we all become one.

A sloth moves slow, such a goofy show,
While frogs leap high, in a wild flow.
Laughter echoes through the trees,
Nature's jokes, carried on the breeze.

Ruby Red Papaya

A papaya fell from a tree with a thud,
I slipped right in, landing with a dud.
The juice splashed out, bright and bold,
Turning my day from bland to gold.

With each sweet bite, my worries fade,
The birds all chirp, 'What a grand parade!'
I wear my fruit hat, so very chic,
In this fruity world, I feel so unique.

In the Shade of Banyan Trees

Beneath branches wide, a hammock swings,
I nap with bugs, oh the joy it brings.
A lizard crawls by, with quite the flair,
While squirrels gossip about who's a bear.

In this cool spot, the world feels light,
With breezy laughter, it's quite the sight.
I share my snack with a cheeky rat,
Together we giggle, imagine that!

Juicy Hues of Summer

Under the sun, we chase the ice cream,
Watching the drips, a melting dream.
Lemons and mangoes, colors so bright,
The taste of summer, such pure delight.

Splashing in puddles, we sing loud and free,
With watermelon slices, shared happily.
Silly hats wobble on our heads,
Laughter and sunburns, our summer threads.

Shades of Paradise in Every Sip

Coconut water's all the rage,
Sipping it like a beach-bound sage.
Pineapples twirl in a fruit parade,
Adding sweetness to every charade.

Mango madness, oh what a delight,
Just don't let it dribble, that could be a fright.
Lemons laughing, stealing the show,
While limes are giving it all a glow.

Strawberry daiquiris, party's on fire,
With every sip, our laughter climbs higher.
And if the blender starts to shake,
We joyfully brace for the fruity quake.

In this oasis, we pour and we share,
Liquid sunshine fills the air.
With every glass, we toast and cheer,
For the joy of flavors, and a hearty beer.

Harvest Moon Over Eden's Ingredients

Under the moon, we gather round,
With spices and fruits that joyfully astound.
Tomatoes giggling, cilantro too,
Dancing in bowls, just me and you.

Pumpkins prancing beneath the stars,
They're plotting mischief in the night's jars.
Chilis are winking, hot and bold,
While garlic laughs, its stories untold.

Onions are slicing through the night air,
While avocados have no single care.
Limes join the jive, squeezing their zest,
Whipping up flavors that truly impress.

As dishes come forth, we dive in with glee,
Each bite a burst of sheer jubilee.
We savor the moon's radiant glow,
Creating our feast with a cheeky flow.

Island Symphony

The ukulele strums a saucy tune,
As coconuts sway like a hot afternoon.
Bananas chuckle as they hang out high,
While papayas giggle at a passing piñata sky.

Flip-flops flapping, we dance with flair,
Dancing on sand, without a care.
And if the tide brings in kelp to greet,
We just laugh louder and tap our feet.

The fish are finned, swimming in time,
With flavors so bold, they almost rhyme.
A symphony of tastes across the shore,
Each dish a joke, begging for more.

So let's sip rum from coconut shells,
In this vibrant place where laughter dwells.
With shouts of joy, we wave goodbye,
To the worries of land, and let spirits fly.

Sun-Kissed Reflections

On golden beaches, the sun shines bright,
Reflections glimmer, a hilarious sight.
Wet hair bouncing with every splash,
As friends share snacks from a funky stash.

Chips and salsa, the crunch is real,
With guacamole that elicits a squeal.
Tropical fruit salad spins with pride,
As mango makes a splash, just like a tide.

A hammock sways, giggles take flight,
While seagulls squawk, adding to the light.
Sunburned noses and sunhats askew,
We take a fruity drink, just me and you.

As the sun sets, casting a glow,
Our laughter echoes, and off we go.
Each moment's a treasure, no chance for regrets,
With sun-kissed smiles and colorful pets.

Lush Green Veils

In a jungle where the monkeys swing,
A parrot shouts, 'I can't sing!'
Beneath the leaves where wild things dance,
An iguana stares, it missed its chance.

A sloth hangs low, enjoying a snack,
'What's this?' he groans, 'No time to slack!'
With his slow-mo groove and a leafy coat,
He'll nap on a branch, in his sleepy boat.

Plates of Tropical Rituals

On plates piled high with fruit and bliss,
A pineapple winks, 'You can't resist!'
Mangoes flirt with their juicy cheer,
While a coconut laughs, 'I'm the crack-up here!'

Bananas slip, making a show,
'You'll need some help,' they cheerfully crow.
In this feast, there's joy and fun,
Even the papaya says, 'Let's be one!'

The Sound of Distant Drums

Beat, clap, on the sand they play,
The crabs can't keep pace, they scurry away!
A turtle taps, with style so rare,
'Let's move it, my friends, without a care!'

As drums get loud, the waves join in,
A fish comes dancing, thinks it can win.
But the seaweed sways, making it a brawl,
'Hey, take it easy! Not a free-for-all!'

Silhouette of Coconut Trees

Coconut trees cast shadows at dusk,
With squirrels above, it's all quite brusque.
They chatter and chatter, in witty debate,
'Who'll stay up late? Or is it too great?'

They play hide and seek, their stash up high,
While the sea breezes sing a lullaby.
Floating in laughter, the night peeks through,
'Trees aren't that slow, they've got thoughts too!'

Coral Caress

In waters where the fish laugh loud,
Bubble-blowers, a giggling crowd.
The crabs dance with their silly flair,
Underneath the sun's warm stare.

Seaweed tickles, a funny scene,
Jellyfish waltz, all smooth and green.
Octopus jokes with eight-armed grace,
In this underwater, joyful place.

A turtle laughs with a wobbly grin,
While seahorses twirl and spin.
The corals chuckle, a riotous hue,
In their reef of wonders, oh so true.

So if you wander where water's bright,
Join the fun, from morning to night.
Laughter bubbles, in every wave,
For nature's humor, it's what we crave.

The Breeze's Secret

Whispers of laughter, the breeze spills low,
It sneaks through the trees, oh what a show!
Parrots gossip, with feathers so bright,
Tickling the air, a delightful flight.

Palm fronds sway to the wind's little jokes,
Shells on the beach hold stories from folks.
The sun winks slyly, a friendly tease,
As flip-flops dance with the teasing breeze.

Coconuts roll, a game they choose,
Finding their way, just like a ruse.
With each gust that breezes by,
We chuckle along as the seagulls fly.

So when you hear that playful sigh,
Know the breeze is laughing, oh my, oh my!
Join in the fun, let your spirits soar,
In a world where laughter is never a bore.

Vibrant Petals and Playful Tides

Flowers giggle in colors so bright,
Tickling each other, what a sight!
Sunflowers grin, their faces wide,
While daisies dance, with petals as pride.

The rain drops come with a splashy cheer,
Each droplet brings fun, don't you fear.
Petals skip like kids in a race,
On waves of laughter, they find their place.

Breezes tease blossoms, a swirling game,
With every gust, they shout their name.
Bees buzz in, curious and bold,
Wagging their tales, with stories told.

In this garden, joy is cultivated,
With each bloom, laughter is celebrated.
Join the petals, let your heart glide,
In a world of color, where smiles abide.

A Journey Through Mango Meadows

In mango fields where laughter grows,
Fruits burst forth, a sweet repose.
Ticklish breezes, tickle the trees,
With quirky tales that float with ease.

Juicy bites, oh what a treat,
Sticky fingers from head to feet.
Every munch a giggle escape,
In summer's embrace, we all take shape.

Mangoes tumble, rolling away,
Chasing each other in a silly ballet.
The truck's honk laughs, the driver grins,
As we savor the joy, where flavor begins.

So pack your bags for a fruity ride,
With giggles and smiles, let's glide.
In mango meadows, so sweet and fun,
The journey's just ending, but joy's begun.

Island Warmth

The sun's a grill, I feel so fried,
A coconut's my best friend, oh my,
I dive for fruit, not pearls at sea,
Oranges roll away, laughing at me.

The sand is hot, I do the hop,
Trying to find a shaded stop,
A crab stole my flip-flop, oh dear!
This island life is quite the cheer!

A seagull squawks a cheeky tune,
As I sip juice with a little spoon,
My hair's a mess like seaweed blown,
But here on the beach, I feel at home!

With ice cream melting on my nose,
And fish that dance in flowing prose,
I trip on waves and laugh so loud,
This sunny life makes me so proud!

Secrets of Calypso

Calypso beat, it's all awhirl,
The pineapple's got moves, let it twirl,
I take a sip, it's too much zest,
But I won't stop, I'm on a quest!

The locals laugh, they join the song,
As conch shells honk, it won't take long,
My dance is slick, though my foot's a mess,
I slip on rum, what a funny dress!

Chasing parrots, wearing a grin,
I thought I caught one, but it was a tin,
They squawk the tales of sunset skies,
While I just try not to eat their fries!

With every beat, I lose my shame,
The ocean whispers, calls my name,
And in this place where laughter flows,
The secrets of Calypso, nobody knows!

Coral Reef Visions

Underwater dreams, I float with glee,
A fish winked at me, was that a plea?
The coral giggles, tickling my toes,
In this strange land where laughter grows.

The octopus plays checkers with me,
While turtles gossip, oh dear, can't flee,
I stumble on shells, a hilarious sight,
Dressed in seaweed, I just might take flight!

A crab offers me a sea cucumber,
I politely refuse, oh, what a bummer!
With bubbles bursting, my snickers rise,
I swear I'm seeing fish in disguise!

The colors swirl in a dance of cheer,
Each wave brings tales that I want to hear,
In this grand reef, where giggles play,
Every splash says, 'Come on, stay!'

Celestial Beach

Stars above, like jellybeans bright,
I stumble on sand, what a funny sight!
The moon winks down, 'Let's have some fun!'
I trip on air, I think I've won!

The tide rolls in, a playful tease,
As waves crash down, I lose my keys,
The conch shells laugh, oh what a crowd,
While I just dance, feeling quite proud!

Fireflies twirl in the warm night air,
As I trip over toes, without a care,
A starfish rolls by, slow and grand,
Saying, "Join the fun! Come take my hand!"

It's not just a shore, it's a giggling spree,
Where every wave sings a song to me,
So here I stay, with my childish delight,
On this celestial beach, the stars shine bright!

A Touch of Pineapple and Spice

The pineapple wore a funny hat,
Dancing around, oh imagine that!
Spices joined in a merry tune,
Chasing each other under the moon.

Ginger gave a little twirl,
While cinnamon made the flag unfurl.
They all laughed at the clumsy lime,
Who rolled away in a fruit-filled mime.

Chili peppers burst with glee,
Inevitably splattering tea.
The flavor parade marched right on,
Creating quirks and smiles till dawn.

Paradise Found in Every Bite

In a coconut shell, a party was tossed,
Where everything sweet had not been lost.
Bananas played cards with a pear,
While mangoes tried hard to comb their hair.

Every nibble was filled with jest,
Like pudding in a pineapple chest.
The avocado hummed a funny tune,
While berries danced under the afternoon.

Lime frolicked in a jelly jar,
As everyone cheered from afar.
In paradise, flavors twist and scream,
Serving up laughter like a dream!

The Language of Tropical Flora

The flowers chatted in wild delight,
Comparing colors from morning to night.
Hibiscus bragged of her vibrant flair,
While orchids blushed with their toxic air.

Petunias giggled at the sun's bright grin,
While daisies danced with a lonesome tin.
Rumors flew from blossom to sprout,
About the spices they couldn't live without.

Every petal told a jolly tale,
Of summer storms and a fruity gale.
In nature's language, they found a way,
To brighten up the dampest day.

Rhythms of a Cascading River

The river sang a bubbly tune,
Trickling along like a happy loon.
It tickled the rocks, making them smile,
As fish danced by in a watery style.

With a splash and a giggle, the current played,
Turning pebbles into a cascade parade.
Mangoes floated, feeling quite spry,
While coconuts jostled and waved goodbye.

The rhythm echoed through the trees,
As parrots joined with a playful breeze.
Every sip was a burst of fun,
A tropical party under the sun!

Vivid Colors of the Horizon

The sun wore shades of peach and gold,
While clouds played hide and seek so bold.
A parrot danced upon a palm,
Sipping coconut drink, feeling calm.

Bananas flipped like acrobats,
Mangoes laughed, bouncing like cats.
The ocean sang, a cheeky tune,
While dolphins twirled beneath the moon.

Grasshoppers sang in a lively beat,
As pineapples set up their street treat.
Coconuts whispered secrets sweet,
While lizards strut on their tiny feet.

In this world where colors explode,
Everything's funny on this bright road.
With each bright hue, a giggle spreads,
Join the fun, forget your dreads!

Nectar of the Island Spirits

Rum and laughter fill the air,
As coconuts wobble in a funny pair.
The tiki torches dance with glee,
While sand crabs do a wobbly spree.

Pineapple skirts and jellybean hats,
The locals sip from colorful vats.
Lime-green frogs croak a jolly tune,
While sunsets turn into a cartoon.

Strawberry piña coladas swirl,
As funny fish around us twirl.
The sun dips low, a cheeky wink,
As dolphins laugh, we clink and drink.

In this land of fruity delight,
Every sip's a pure delight.
Raise your glass, let joy ignite,
Nectar of spirits, pure and bright!

Serengeti of Citrus Hues

Oranges roam the sunset plains,
While lemons dance in silly chains.
Grapefruits call the wild to play,
In their juicy, zesty ballet.

Lime squirrels hop from tree to tree,
Chewing gum with endless glee.
A tangerine twirled with flair,
Donning a crown made of citrus air.

The sun was a giant peach balloon,
Bouncing jokes to the whimsical moon.
With every citrus, a chuckle rose,
As limes posed with a silly nose.

So come explore this vibrant spree,
Where fruits dance wild and free!
In the land of citrus hues,
Laughter's the only thing you lose!

Songs of the Ocean's Palette

Waves giggle, splashing with cheer,
As seafoam tickles, oh so near.
Starfish hum a catchy song,
While crabs scuttle along, so strong.

Coral reefs in their neon dress,
Sing ballads of a silly mess.
Every splash holds a joke untold,
As tides sway to the rhythm bold.

Seagulls squawk in a comic way,
Stealing fries from kids at play.
Octopuses juggle all they can,
Bubbles burst, making a funny plan.

With each wave a merry tune,
As shells and fish dance to the moon.
Join the fun beneath the sky,
Where laughter flows and spirits fly!

Gusts of Joy

A parrot squawks, it's out of tune,
Dancing with the breeze, under the moon.
Palm trees wave, like they want to sway,
As coconut drinks spill on a sunny day.

Flip-flops flying, on the sandy shore,
Someone's lost a shoe; oh, what a chore!
Laughter echoes, as the waves play tag,
And a beach ball bounces, it's all a gag.

Sunburned noses, they shine so bright,
A sun hat flies off, oh what a sight!
Seagulls dive-bomb; they think they're slick,
Stealing fries right off a picnic stick.

So grab your shades, let's dance around,
In this paradise, silliness is found!
With friends and laughter, the fun won't stop,
In this quirky, bright, tropical hop!

Tropic Harvest

Mangoes tumbling, oh what a mess,
Squishy and juicy, they leave a dress.
Hibiscus tea spills over the side,
As a witty crab takes a funny slide.

Bananas laugh, they slip with pride,
As surfers ride waves, with joy as their guide.
Coconuts cracking, what a loud cheer,
The fruit's gone rogue, it's party time, dear!

Limes wear sunglasses, so cool and bright,
While pineapples plot a dance in the night.
A sweet parade of flavors and fun,
In this tropical harvest, there's always a pun.

So join the fiesta, don't be aloof,
Let's taste a rainbow, get on the groove!
With laughter and cheer, it's good for the soul,
In this fruity world, we're all on a roll!

Sweet Escape

Pack your bags with sunscreen and glee,
We're off to a place where we can be free.
Flip-flops fly as the plane takes flight,
Wave goodbye to worries, it feels just right.

In the tropics, the piña coladas flow,
While the sunscreen battles the sun's fierce glow.
A hammock sways, it's time for a nap,
But a crab steals the blanket—what a mishap!

Fish are sardines, they wiggle and laugh,
As a turtle attempts a slow-motion craft.
Sandcastles crumble, but who even cares?
We'll just build giants, with extravagant flares!

So let's escape, let's laugh till we cry,
With fruity delights and the bright blue sky.
At sunset, we'll dance, it's a riotous scene,
In our sweet escape, life's a fun machine!

Footprints in the Sand

Footprints leading to a coconut stand,
Where laughter echoes, it's all so grand.
A dog steals a snack; oh, what a chase,
In this sandy playground, we've found our place.

Each step is a story, a giggle, a slip,
Twirling in circles, let the fun rip.
The sun takes a bow, as it dips down low,
While kids build towers with shells in tow.

A hermit crab races, it's quite the sight,
As we cheer like tourists, pure delight!
Ocean whispers secrets, in salty embrace,
While the footprints vanish, without a trace.

But memories linger, like waves on the shore,
In our heart's little albums, there's always more.
So let's frolic and play, till the last sandy light,
In this comical tale, everything feels right!

Sunlit Adventures Beneath Canopies

Under the palm, I found a snack,
A coconut flew, reminding me of whack!
The sunbeam danced, a golden slide,
I tripped on sand, a funny ride!

Lizards laugh, they wear a grin,
While I'm stuck with a sunscreen bin!
The ocean teased, 'Come take a dive',
I thrived on splashes, the birds did jive!

With flip-flops missing, I run amok,
Jumping like a gal in a mud-filled sock!
The waves they rolled, a bubbly cheer,
I'll catch that fish, just not this year!

Each sun-drenched hour a comic feat,
With every blunder, I'd take a seat.
So raise a toast to this folly spree,
In the tropic sun, I'm wild and free!

Banquets of the Coastal Breeze

A banquet spread on sandy trails,
With fish that laughed and told me tales.
The guac was green, like limes on ice,
I slipped and slid, oh, what a vice!

Tropical fruits, they rolled away,
I chased them down, like kids at play!
A mango winked, the guava smiled,
'C'mon, join us, it's coconut styled!'

A parrot squawked, 'What's on your plate?'
I served him salsa, it's never late.
Got rice on my shirt, it looks like art,
At this coastal feast, I'm playing smart!

With laughter echoing through the breeze,
The day unfolds with silly ease.
A feast of fun, let's not delay,
In every bite, the jokes do play!

Festivities Under the Coconut Canopy

Underneath the leafy crown,
I danced like a clown, wearing a frown.
Pineapples shook, to a reggae beat,
While coconuts rolled with nimble feet!

The drinks were silly, with tiny straws,
I spilled my punch, just because!
The sunbeams giggled, the breeze lent a hand,
In this wild fiesta, my heart took a stand!

Friends flipped and flopped in a conga line,
Tripping on toes, oh what a sign!
With laughter and snacks in endless supply,
We cheered for the night as stars filled the sky!

The coconut canopy, a riot of cheer,
With each silly dance, we erased every fear.
In this universe, we thrive and cope,
With each joyful moment, we're full of hope!

Rainbow Fruits in Sunset Glow

The sunset glimmers with fruity delight,
A rainbow spreads, what a colorful sight!
Watermelons giggled, bananas blushed,
I tripped again, oh, the world was crushed!

With grapes that sang and apples that danced,
Each fruit seemed eager for a wild chance.
Pineapples pranced, on a table spread,
While I took a tumble, landed on my head!

The laughter echoed at this fruity fair,
As I wore a garland of mango hair.
Berry pies wobbled, giving me a fright,
But oh how I chuckled, oh what a sight!

So let's sip tropical drinks by the pier,
With every mistake, we bring on the cheer.
In this sunset glow, we'll dine with flair,
With fruits and giggles, a joyful affair!

Tropical Canvas

Bright parrots laugh in the trees,
Dancing in the warm, sweet breeze.
Coconuts roll, making a fuss,
As we giggle, join the circus!

Fruits so vibrant, wild and bold,
Mangoes laughing, stories told.
We juggle papayas, what a sight,
In this carnival of delight!

Even the sun wears shades so cool,
While lizards lounge, breaking the rule.
Tanned tourists slip on banana peels,
Joy abounds with sunny squeals!

In this place where the sea meets land,
We build our dreams just like we planned.
With laughter echoing through the night,
Our canvas painted in sheer delight.

Symphony of Color and Light

In a garden where colors collide,
Flamboyant blooms take a fun ride.
The butterflies dance, a motley crew,
While bees buzz and play peekaboo!

A parrot squawks a silly tune,
Underneath a goofy moon.
The hibiscus winks, it's a sight!
Join the fun, it's pure delight!

Colors pop like confetti pressed,
This sunny palette feels like a jest.
Palm trees sway, telling their jokes,
As waves chuckle with the sunlit folks!

Even the sunset joins in the cheer,
Painting the sky, bringing us near.
With laughter ringing out of sight,
Life's a symphony, glowing bright!

Hibiscus and Honey

Hibiscus blooms sip morning light,
Wearing their hats, oh what a sight!
Bees in bow ties, buzzing with zest,
Mixing sweet nectar, they're the best!

Honey drips like golden rain,
While flowers tease and slow our gain.
A hummingbird's giggle, oh so sly,
Zooming past like a blush in the sky!

Picnics laid with silly snacks,
Mango slices and jelly quacks.
The sun shines down, a mischievous face,
As we savor smiles in this sweet place!

With each laugh and every cheer,
Nature croons, 'Come join me here!'
Life's a treasure, bold and funny,
With hibiscus grace and drops of honey!

The Tides of Memory

The ocean waves whisper a tale,
Of sandy castles that never fail.
Children giggle, chasing the tide,
As seaweed tangles, letting them ride!

Seagulls squawk with comic flair,
Snatching snacks from unaware.
Beach balls bounce—a playful race,
As friends tumble in this sunny space!

Time drinks in this salty air,
Each wave brings laughter, light as a hare.
In flip-flops slipping with every stride,
We dance like seaweed on the tide!

Mango sunsets, goofy and bright,
Send us home with hearts in flight.
These tides of joy in memory stored,
Remind us always to press 'record!'

Coconut Serenade

Underneath a palm tree's shade,
Coconuts fall like hand grenades.
I duck and dodge, it's quite a sight,
As laughter rings from day to night.

Sipping juice with a silly grin,
Every drop spills on my chin.
The seagulls steal my fruity snack,
Then shrug as if to say, "What's lack?"

When it rains, the coconuts sway,
Bouncing rhythm, come what may.
I dance along with sandy feet,
Pretending I'm the star of this beat.

So let the breeze pipe a tune,
As I twirl beneath the moon.
Coconuts have all the fun,
Next time, I'll stay under the sun.

The Dance of Sea Breezes

Oh the wind, it likes to tease,
Tugging hats and flicking leaves.
I chase my flip-flops down the shore,
While the ocean dances, I implore.

With every gust, I feel alive,
Like a kite, I just might dive.
But caught in waves of salty spray,
I shout, "I'm not a fish today!"

The surf is laughing, what a show,
As my beach ball makes a getaway flow.
I chase it down with much dismay,
"O beach ball, do come back and play!"

Yet in the chaos, joy persists,
As I tumble in the ocean mist.
A dance with breezes, no mishap,
Just me and laughter in my cap.

Nature's Exotic Palette

In gardens where the colors gleam,
Flowers bloom, a painter's dream.
It's a party for the bees,
Buzzing 'round with utmost ease.

Mangoes plop and pineapples roll,
I grab one quick, oh what a goal!
But slippery fruits have other plans,
Lost my grip like a pair of hands.

Bouncing fruits and sneaky vines,
Nature's jokes in playful lines.
As I dance with the quirky flora,
I trip on roots, "What a chora!"

So here's to colors wild and free,
And fruit that says, "Come laugh with me!"
I plunge into this painted spree,
Where every hue says, "Just be me!"

Lush Canopy Echoes

In the jungle, oh what fun,
Every leaf is like a pun.
Monkey chatter filled with glee,
"Join our party, swing with me!"

Parrots squawk in technicolor,
While lizards slide with such a flutter.
I stumble on a vine so thick,
And fall with style, oh what a trick!

The peacocks strut with flair and grace,
They pose for selfies, what a face!
In this lush, wild, chaotic show,
Nature's humor begins to flow.

So let's embrace the jungle's quirk,
With every laugh, let's go berserk.
In this green world, oh what a spree,
Let the canopy echo with our decree!

Secrets of the Surfing Tide

The wave took my hat, oh what a sight,
A seagull laughed, flying left and right.
I tried to surf, but fell with a splash,
Sand in my shorts, now that's a real clash!

With coconut drinks, I danced on the shore,
Only to drop them; they rolled, what a chore!
A crab came to join, intent on a snack,
He nibbled my toe, then scuttled back!

The sun was bright, and so was my skin,
I looked like a lobster; where to begin?
Everyone laughed, it was quite the scene,
Life at the beach, we live like a dream.

But when the tide rolled in, I saw the thrill,
A fish with a grin lost my flip-flop still.
Yet here on the sand, with friends all around,
We laughed through the waves, joy truly profound.

Embracing the Tide's Caress

Oh, the waves they whisper, a silly old tale,
Of mermaids with drinks that always turn stale.
I paddled so hard, fell into a whirl,
Spitting out water and quite a few pearls!

A beach ball floated, it looked just like me,
Rolling past sunbathers without a decree.
I chased it so far; it danced like a sprite,
But forgot to check the tide, what a fright!

My sunscreen was rogue, I smeared it on thick,
Now I look like a hot dog, this is my trick!
Everyone giggled, "What color is that?"
A glowing red beacon, imagine a brat!

We danced with the tide, sang songs to the sun,
Every slip and trip made it all the more fun.
With laughter and joy, we embraced the glee,
Life's funny like this, just come and see!

Lively Markets of Exotic Wonder

The market was bustling, colors galore,
I tried to barter, they laughed, wanting more.
I offered a smile, then tripped on a shoe,
Adventurers giggling, all cheering, "Woo-hoo!"

Fruits piled high, like a rainbow so bright,
I picked up a mango, it flew like a kite.
The vendor just shrugged, his eyes wide with cheer,
Throw the fruit back, and I'll make you a spear!

A bird in the corner was eyeing my treats,
I braved the odd looks and shared him some sweets.
He squawked and he hopped, high fives we exchanged,
In this lively market, the vibes felt so strange!

But here came the rain, while I danced with the stalls,
Umbrellas went flying, we laughed through the brawls.
What fun in the chaos, what joy in dispute,
Life's lively and bright, a tropical hoot!

Journey Through Tropical Aromas

The scent of piña coladas in the air,
I tripped on my flip-flops, without a care.
The fruit stalls beckoned, a feast for the nose,
I grabbed a fine mango, but it slipped—oh no!

With each fruity taste, a giggle would burst,
I chewed too fast, and all flavors dispersed.
The laughter behind me only made me grin,
Did they just capture my mango-smeared chin?

A spice stand nearby sent me into a whirl,
I tasted a spice that made my eyes twirl.
The vendor just chuckled, "A hot one, my friend,
In tropical realms, the laughter won't end!"

So here's to the flavors, the laughter, the cheer,
Let's toast to this journey, with friends gathered near.
Let's savor the fun and all that's in store,
For in every sweet moment, we're longing for more!

www.ingramcontent.com/pod-product-compliance
Lightning Source LLC
Chambersburg PA
CBHW072123070526
44585CB00016B/1540